EARLY TO LATER INTERMEDIATE

ROMANTIC REFLECTIONS

8 ORIGINAL PIANO SOLOS

by Carolyn C. Setliff

ISBN 978-1-4768-8955-9

EXCLUSIVELY DISTRIBUTED BY

HAL•LEONARD®
CORPORATION
7777 W. BLUEMOUND RD. P.O. BOX 13819
MILWAUKEE, WISCONSIN 53213

Visit Hal Leonard Online at
www.halleonard.com

FROM THE COMPOSER

It has been such a pleasure to compose these pieces. I find that the romantic style very much lends itself to individual interpretation, and many of these pieces were written with a particular student in mind. Melodious music always brings back warm memories of childhood, as I grew up in a home that was constantly filled with music. One memory is of my first Chopin waltz in B minor (op. 69, no. 2). It was assigned when I was 12 years old, and I was thrilled.

As a singer, I instinctively listen for the melodic line. Shaping the melodic phrases and paying careful attention to dynamic markings will take the performance to a higher level. Remember that each dynamic marking allows for some variation in volume, and within each section, just a subtle rise and fall of the melodic line will add much beauty.

It is always exciting to hear students perform my pieces. Each one is special to me. Feel free to put your own personality into these pieces and to let the music inspire you to be creative and expressive. It is my hope that one or more of these solos will bring you joy as you learn and perform and give them your own unique touch.

My appreciation to David Engle, retired Willis editor, who edited "Whispers of Dawn," "Promises," and "Romantic Serenade" when they were originally published, and to Charmaine Siagian, my current editor—her input and encouragement have been most helpful.

Carolyn C. Sutliff

CONTENTS

Whispers of Dawn

for Melissa Levina

Carolyn C. Setliff

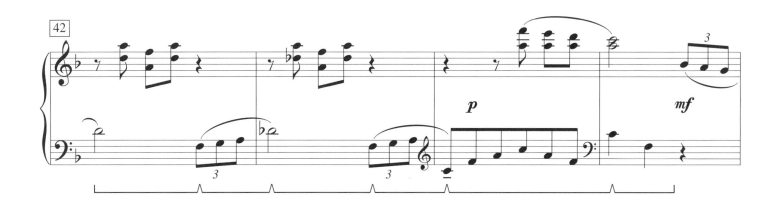

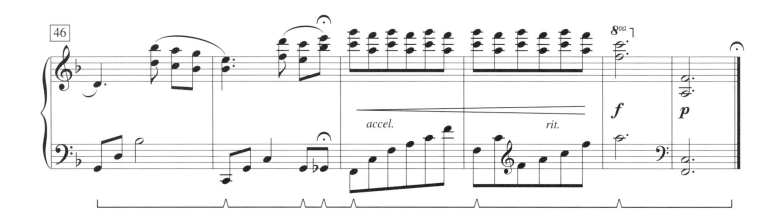

Promises

for Cathy Dawson

Carolyn C. Setliff

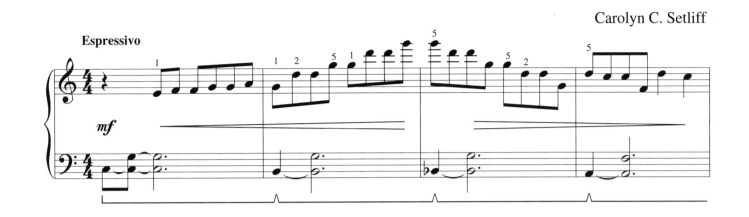

Poème

for Franchesca Lau

Carolyn C. Setliff

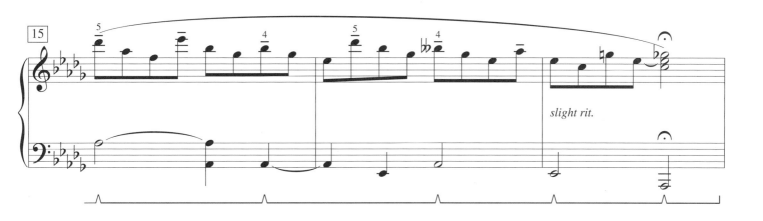

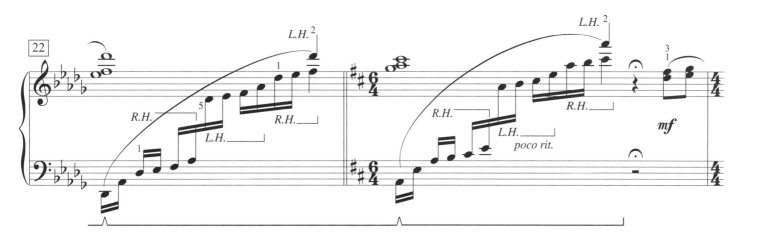

Sunset Splendor

Carolyn C. Setliff

With dignity

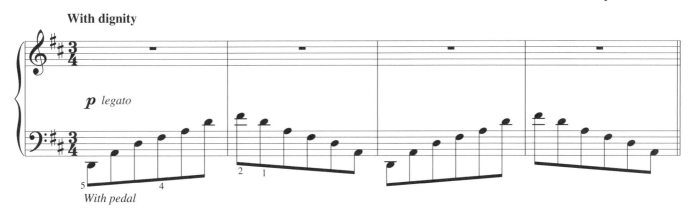

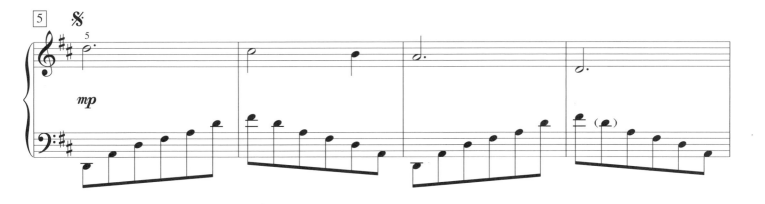

Midnight Nocturne

Carolyn C. Setliff

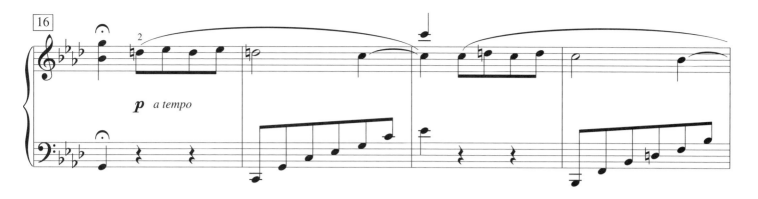

Romantic Serenade

for Lamar

Carolyn C. Setliff

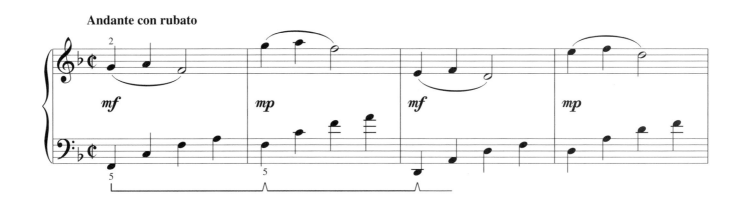

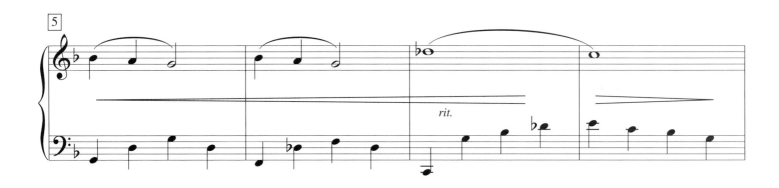

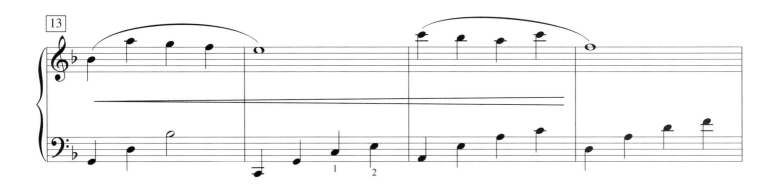

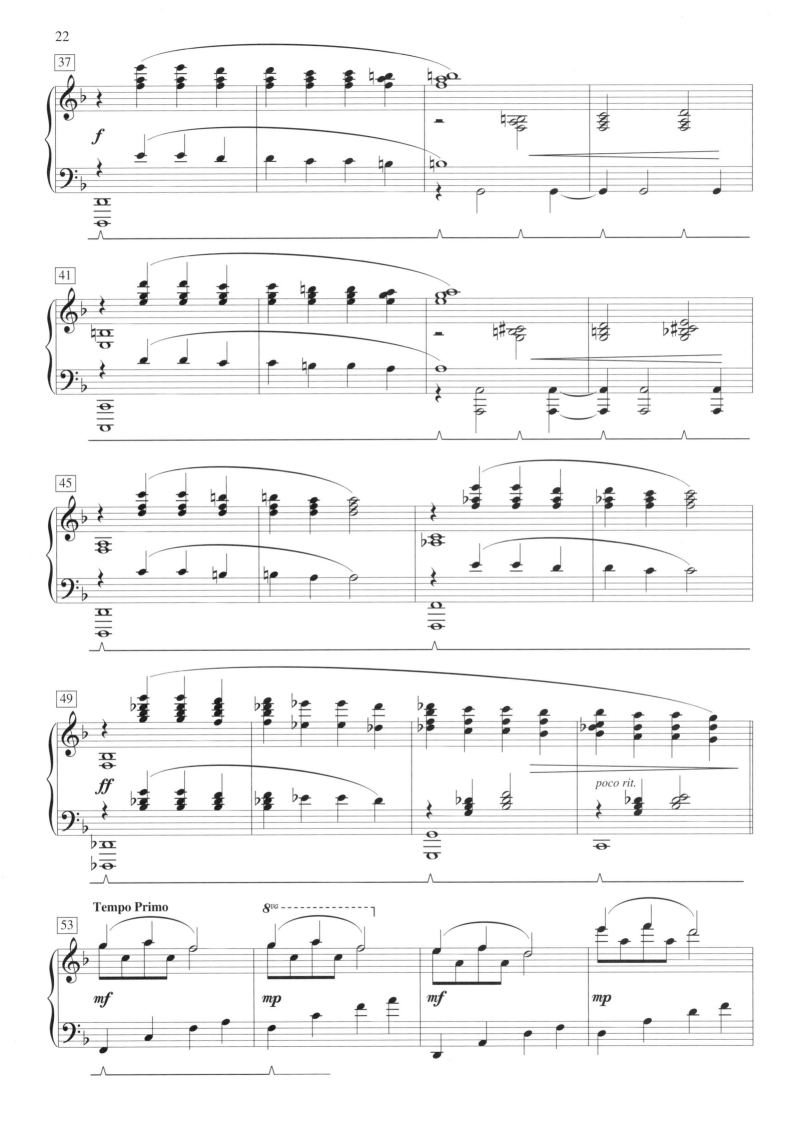

Romantic Reflections

for Elizabeth

Carolyn C. Setliff

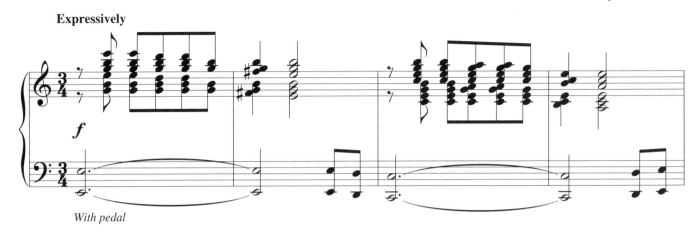

Intermezzo in D-flat Major

Carolyn C. Setliff

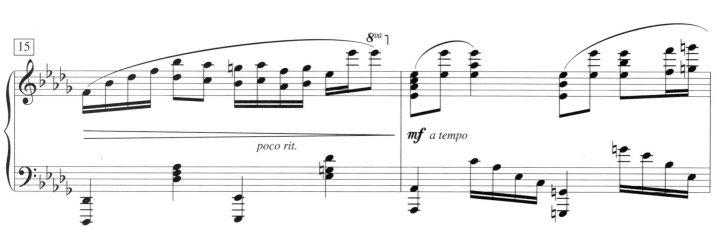

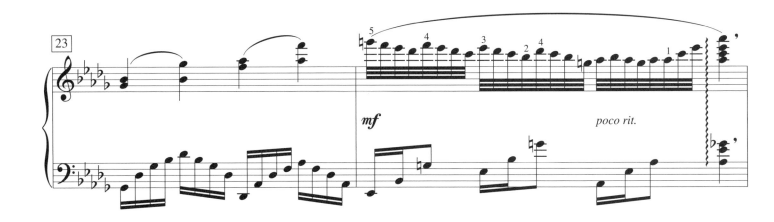

BIOGRAPHY

Composer **Carolyn C. Setliff** lives in Little Rock, Arkansas. She writes, "Music is such an important part of my life. My mother was a piano teacher and a church organist, and my twin sister and I followed in her footsteps. She and I sang in church and school choirs, played in piano recitals, accompanied, performed, and studied piano throughout childhood and through to college. Now my daughter also teaches piano!"

Currently, her home studio consists of 30 students aged 7 to 17. "They inspire me, challenge me, and make me laugh!" Carolyn is an active member of the local, state, and national music teacher associations, and a regular adjudicator at piano festivals and composition competitions. She also presents workshops on composing and teaching.

In her spare time, Carolyn loves to read, spend time with her grandchildren, and travel.